Collins

easy learning

Times tables bumper book

Ages 7-11

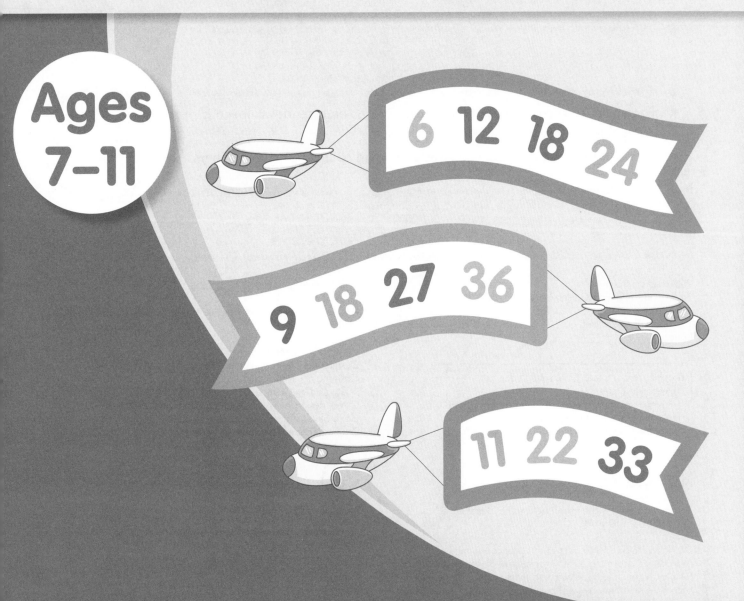

Simon Greaves

How to use this book

- Easy Learning bumper books help your child improve basic skills, build confidence and develop a love of learning.

- Find a quiet, comfortable place to work, away from distractions.

- Get into a routine of completing one or two bumper book pages with your child every day.

- Ask your child to circle the star that matches how many questions they have completed every two pages:

Some = half of the questions Most = more than half All = all the questions

- The progress certificate at the back of this book will help you and your child keep track of how many have been circled.

- Encourage your child to work through all of the questions eventually, and praise them for completing the progress certificate.

- The ability to recall and use times tables facts is an essential skill and is invaluable for many mathematical processes.

- Learning tables at an early age gives your child confidence with numbers.

Parent tip
Look out for tips on how to help your child learn tables.

Published by Collins
An imprint of HarperCollins*Publishers* Ltd
The News Building
1 London Bridge Street
London
SE1 9GF

Browse the complete Collins catalogue at
www.collins.co.uk

© HarperCollins*Publishers* Ltd 2011
This edition © HarperCollins*Publishers* Ltd 2015

10 9 8 7 6

ISBN 978-0-00-815149-2

British Library Cataloguing in Publication Data.

A Catalogue record for this publication is available from the British Library.

Written by Simon Greaves
Design and layout by Linda Miles, Lodestone Publishing and Contentra Technologies Ltd
Illustrated by Graham Smith and Jenny Tulip
Cover design by Sarah Duxbury and Paul Oates
Cover illustration © Shutterstock.com/Yayayoyo
Project managed by Sonia Dawkins

FSC
www.fsc.org

MIX
Paper from responsible source
FSC™ C007454

This book is produced from independently certified FSC™ paper to ensure responsible forest management.

For more information visit:
www.harpercollins.co.uk/green

Contents

Six times table

1 The answers to a multiplication table are called multiples.
Put a circle around the numbers that are multiples of 6.

36	12	21	43
	18	57	66	42

2 Work out the answer to each multiplication to complete the table.
Use the code to replace each number with the correct letter in the word below.

What is the word?

_____

4 × 6		n
6 × 6		r
1 × 6		a
9 × 6		b
2 × 6		l
5 × 6		i
3 × 6		t

☐ ☐ ☐ ☐ ☐ ☐ ☐ ☐ ☐ !

54   36   30   12   12   30   6   24   18

3 A DVD costs £6.
How much will it cost to buy:

2 DVDs £ ☐   7 DVDs £ ☐

5 DVDs £ ☐   10 DVDs £ ☐

12 DVDs £ ☐   6 DVDs £ ☐

How many DVDs can you buy for £18? ☐

How many DVDs can you buy for £48? ☐

4 In each line, circle the multiplication that matches the number in the box.

| 18 | 1 × 6 | 4 × 6 | 3 × 6 | 5 × 6 |

| 42 | 2 × 6 | 7 × 6 | 5 × 6 | 6 × 6 |

| 24 | 4 × 6 | 9 × 6 | 6 × 6 | 10 × 6 |

| 48 | 3 × 6 | 7 × 6 | 8 × 6 | 4 × 6 |

Parent tip
Look for answers in the six times table on everyday objects.

5 There are six apples on a tree.
Write a multiplication to show the number of apples on the trees.

☐ × 6 = ☐

☐ × ☐ = ☐

☐ × ☐ = ☐

6 Count on or back in sixes. Fill in the missing numbers.

6	☐	18	☐	30	☐	☐	☐
48	☐	36	☐	☐	18	☐	☐
18	☐	30	36	☐	☐	☐	☐
72	66	☐	☐	☐	☐	36	☐

How much did you do?   Questions 1–6

Circle the star
to show what
you have done.

Some

Most

★
All

Seven times table

1 Write in the missing numbers.

$21 = \boxed{} \times 7$

$\boxed{} = 6 \times 7$

$28 = \boxed{} \times 7$

$\boxed{} = 1 \times 7$

$\boxed{} = 7 \times 7$

$70 = \boxed{} \times 7$

$\boxed{} = 5 \times 7$

$77 = \boxed{} \times 7$

$63 = \boxed{} \times 7$

$\boxed{} = 8 \times 7$

2 Complete the multiplication fact that describes each pattern.

$3 \times 7 = 21$

$\boxed{} \times 7 = \boxed{}$

$\boxed{} \times 7 = \boxed{}$

$\boxed{} \times \boxed{} = \boxed{}$

$\boxed{} \times \boxed{} = \boxed{}$

$\boxed{} \times \boxed{} = \boxed{}$

3 To find the product of two numbers you multiply them together.

Find the product of 2 and 7. $\boxed{}$

Find the product of 6 and 7. $\boxed{}$

What is the product of 4 and 7? $\boxed{}$

What is the product of 12 and 7? $\boxed{}$

Parent tip
Record the seven times table on a media player for your child to listen to and repeat

4 Every number put into the number machine is multiplied by seven.
Fill in the missing numbers.

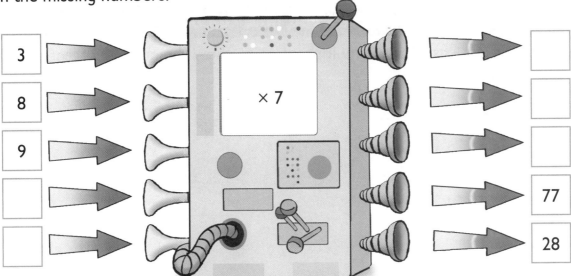

3 →
8 →
9 →
→
→

× 7

→ [ ]
→ [ ]
→ [ ]
→ 77
→ 28

5 Answer these questions:

What is the fifth multiple of seven? [ ]

What is 12 times 7? [ ]

What is nine multiplied by seven? [ ]

What number multiplied by 7 gives 28? [ ]

What is the product of six and seven? [ ]

What are the first three multiples of seven? [ ] [ ] [ ]

6 Colour each square that is an answer in the seven times table.

Which letter of the alphabet do you see?

_____

35	7	70	21	49
17	62	42	31	15
26	29	28	3	51
66	19	56	34	23
69	25	63	11	44
45	20	14	32	67

Eight times table

The eight times table tells you how to count in sets of eight.

1 A spider has eight legs. Write a multiplication to show the number of legs in each group of spiders.

$3 \times 8 =$ ☐

☐ $\times 8 =$ ☐

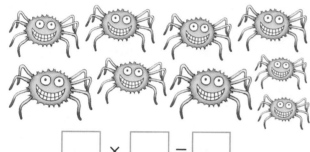

☐ $\times$ ☐ $=$ ☐

☐ $\times$ ☐ $=$ ☐

2 Here are some multiplications. Some are correct and some are not.
Put a tick next to those with the correct answer. ✔
Put a cross next to those with the wrong answer. ✘

$8 \times 8 = 56$ ☐ $5 \times 8 = 40$ ☐ $3 \times 8 = 24$ ☐ $9 \times 8 = 80$ ☐

$11 \times 8 = 88$ ☐ $7 \times 8 = 56$ ☐ $10 \times 8 = 90$ ☐ $4 \times 8 = 32$ ☐

3 Colour a path through the number grid. You may only go through answers that are in the eight times table.

55	33	44	5	96	→ Finish
27	27	36	18	40	
61	17	72	32	64	
3	43	80	6	70	
1	8	56	33	30	
24	16	75	71	2	

Start →

Parent tip
Make a chart for your child to keep track of which eights they know/ need to learn.

4 Complete the multiplication fact that describes each pattern.

$4 \times 8 = 32$

⬜ $\times 8 = $ ⬜

⬜ $\times 8 = $ ⬜

⬜ $\times$ ⬜ $=$ ⬜

⬜ $\times$ ⬜ $=$ ⬜

⬜ $\times$ ⬜ $=$ ⬜

5 Colour multiples of eight in the grid.

What letter do you see?

_____

8	20	7	64
50	48	80	34
31	40	72	46
32	66	25	88

6 Answer these questions.

What is the product of 8 and 6? ⬜

What is 7 times 8? ⬜

Which number multiplied by 8 is 96? ⬜

Multiply eight by itself. ⬜

What is the sixth multiple of eight? ⬜

How many eights are in 32? ⬜

How much did you do?   Questions 1–6

Circle the star to show what you have done.

Some

Most

All

Mixed tables

1 Fill in the missing answers.

$8 \times 3 =$ ☐ $4 \times 6 =$ ☐ $2 \times 3 =$ ☐

$9 \times 6 =$ ☐ $2 \times 6 =$ ☐ $10 \times 3 =$ ☐

$6 \times 3 =$ ☐ $7 \times 3 =$ ☐ $3 \times 3 =$ ☐

$6 \times 6 =$ ☐ $5 \times 3 =$ ☐ $5 \times 6 =$ ☐

$3 \times 6 =$ ☐ $7 \times 6 =$ ☐ $11 \times 6 =$ ☐

$9 \times 3 =$ ☐ $8 \times 6 =$ ☐ $4 \times 3 =$ ☐

2 Write the numbers on the shirts by counting on or back in threes or sixes.

6   24

42   30

12   21

3 Complete the multiplication grid.

×	1	10	3	12	9	7
6						
3						

Parent tip
Time how quickly your child can say the three times table.

4 Complete the times table wheels for the three and six times tables.

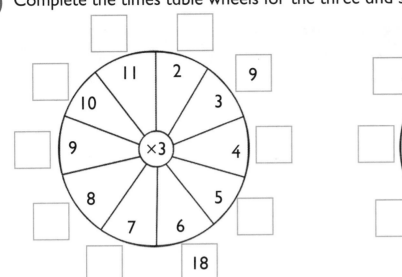

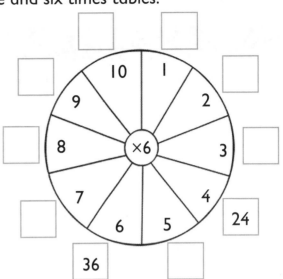

5 Use the three times table facts to work out the answers to the six times table facts.

$1 \times 3 = \quad 3$ $\qquad$ $3 \times 3 = \quad 9$ $\qquad$ $4 \times 3 = \quad 12$

$1 \times 6 = \quad 6$ $\qquad$ $3 \times 6 = \boxed{}$ $\qquad$ $4 \times 6 = \boxed{}$

$6 \times 3 = \quad 18$ $\qquad$ $8 \times 3 = \quad 24$ $\qquad$ $9 \times 3 = \quad 27$

$6 \times 6 = \boxed{}$ $\qquad$ $8 \times 6 = \boxed{}$ $\qquad$ $9 \times 6 = \boxed{}$

6 Find a path through the maze. You can only go through numbers that are multiples of three or six.

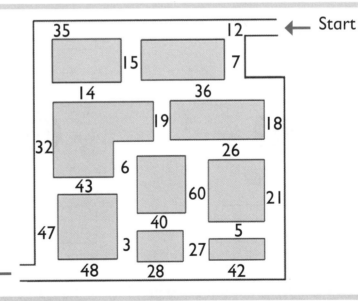

Mixed tables

1 Complete this times table challenge in less than two minutes. Time yourself.

$2 \times 4 =$ ☐ $3 \times 8 =$ ☐ $7 \times 8 =$ ☐ $8 \times 8 =$ ☐

$10 \times 4 =$ ☐ $1 \times 4 =$ ☐ $4 \times 4 =$ ☐ $9 \times 8 =$ ☐

$2 \times 8 =$ ☐ $6 \times 8 =$ ☐ $6 \times 4 =$ ☐ $9 \times 4 =$ ☐

$5 \times 4 =$ ☐ $5 \times 8 =$ ☐ $11 \times 8 =$ ☐ $3 \times 4 =$ ☐

2 Here are some targets.
If an arrow lands in the white ring it scores 4 times the number.
If an arrow lands in the blue ring it scores 8 times the number.
Write down the score for each target.

$3 \times 4 =$ ☐

   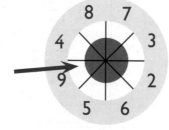   

3 Draw a line to match each product to its correct answer.

$\left(6 \times 4\right)$ $\left(4 \times 4\right)$ $\left(12 \times 4\right)$ $\left(8 \times 8\right)$ $\left(5 \times 8\right)$ $\left(5 \times 4\right)$

(16)   (48)   (40)   (64)   (20)   (24)

4 Work out the answer to the multiplication in each bubble. Find this answer in the numbered boxes below. Write in the letter from that bubble in the space above the box.
What is the hidden message?

6 × 4
U

2 × 4
P

7 × 8
E

8 × 8
N

5 × 4
V

5 × 8
R

4 × 8
G

7 × 4
I

Parent tip
Chant the answers to the four times table forwards and backwards.

												!
64	56	20	56	40		32	28	20	56		24	8

5 Circle the numbers that are answers in both the four and eight times tables.

20   32   22   16   8   14   40   28

6 An adult cinema ticket costs £8.
A child cinema ticket costs £4.

Adult £8   Child £4

How much would it cost to buy:

4 adult tickets?   £ [ ]   11 child tickets?   £ [ ]

5 child tickets?   £ [ ]   7 adult tickets?   £ [ ]

7 child tickets?   £ [ ]   8 adult tickets?   £ [ ]

How much did you do?   ## Questions 1–6

Circle the star to show what you have done.

Some

Most

All

Mixed tables

Sixes, sevens and eights

1 Write the multiplications for the two scores on each dartboard.

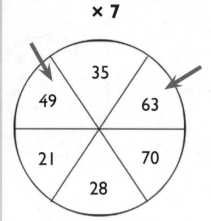

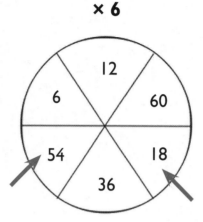

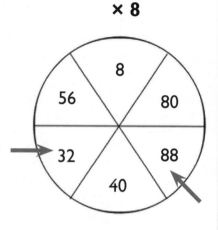

$7 \times 7 = 49$

☐ × ☐ = ☐

☐ × 6 = ☐

☐ × ☐ = ☐

☐ × 8 = ☐

☐ × ☐ = ☐

2 Here are some cards showing different multiples.
Shade red the multiples of six.
Shade blue the multiples of seven.
Shade green the multiples of eight.

Parent tip
Ask your child to recite the six, seven and eight times tables out loud.

64	40	30	54	14	77	12

| 35 | | 21 | | 32 | |

3 Answer these questions.

Find the product of 5 and 6. ☐

Multiply 6 by 8. ☐

What is 9 times 7? ☐

What is 8 multiplied by 8? ☐

What is the product of 8 and 7? ☐

Multiply 12 by 6. ☐

4 Complete the multiplication grid.

×	5		8		12
7		21		42	
8		24		48	
6		18		36	

5 Follow the road each multiplication car will take to reach its parking place.
Write the answer to the multiplication in the correct parking place.

6 Fill in the missing numbers.
See if you can complete them in less than two minutes. Time yourself!

3 × 8 = ☐   ☐ × 7 = 49   9 × ☐ = 72

5 × 6 = ☐   ☐ × 7 = 14   4 × ☐ = 24

3 × 6 = ☐   10 × 6 = ☐   5 × 8 = ☐

☐ × 7 = 56   9 × ☐ = 63   ☐ × 8 = 48

☐ × 6 = 54   1 × 7 = ☐   11 × 6 = ☐

Nine times table

The nine times table tells you how to count in sets of nine.

1 Look at the numbers in the box.
Circle the multiples of nine.

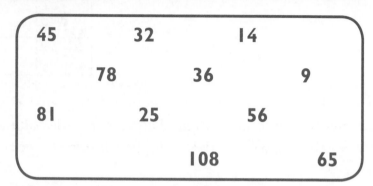

45	32	14
78	36	9
81	25	56
108	65

2 Complete the multiplication fact that describes each pattern.

$\boxed{} \times 9 = \boxed{}$ $\boxed{} \times 9 = \boxed{}$ $\boxed{} \times 9 = \boxed{}$

$\boxed{} \times \boxed{} = \boxed{}$ $\boxed{} \times \boxed{} = \boxed{}$

Parent tip
Make a chart for your child to keep track of which nines they know/need to learn.

3 Choose the correct answer for each multiplication question.
Shade the letter next to that answer.

$3 \times 9 = 27 \boxed{n}$ or $36 \boxed{p}$ $5 \times 9 = 40 \boxed{b}$ or $45 \boxed{i}$

$9 \times 9 = 72 \boxed{o}$ or $81 \boxed{n}$ $4 \times 9 = 36 \boxed{e}$ or $45 \boxed{f}$

$8 \times 9 = 63 \boxed{u}$ or $72 \boxed{t}$ $7 \times 9 = 72 \boxed{m}$ or $63 \boxed{y}$

The letters you have shaded spell out a multiple of nine. What is it? $\boxed{}$

4 Draw a string from each multiplication kite to the box showing the correct answer.

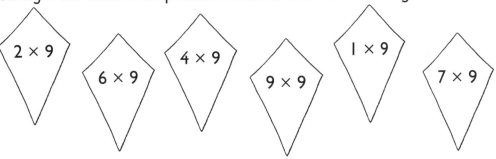

| 2 × 9 | 6 × 9 | 4 × 9 | 9 × 9 | 1 × 9 | 7 × 9 |

| 63 | 36 | 81 | 9 | 18 | 54 |

5 Write the number in the box that multiplies by nine to give the number in the circle.

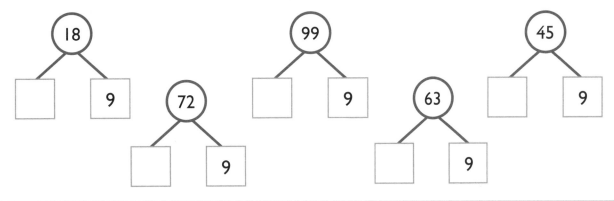

18 — □ 9
72 — □ 9
99 — □ 9
63 — □ 9
45 — □ 9

6 Write the answers to each pair of multiplications on the flowers.
What do you notice about each pair of answers?

_____

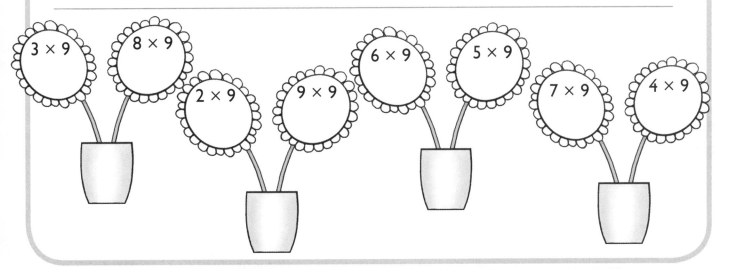

3 × 9   8 × 9   2 × 9   9 × 9   6 × 9   5 × 9   7 × 9   4 × 9

How much did you do?   Questions 1–6

Circle the star to show what you have done.

Some

Most

All

Mixed tables

1 Look at the answer on each calculator.
Write the multiplications by three, six and nine that give that answer.

☐ × 3 = 30

☐ × 6 = 30

☐ × ☐ = ☐

☐ × ☐ = ☐

☐ × ☐ = ☐

☐ × ☐ = ☐

☐ × ☐ = ☐

☐ × ☐ = ☐

2 Answer these questions.

What is 6 times 6? ☐

Multiply three by itself. ☐

What is eleven times six? ☐

Multiply 5 by 9. ☐

Which number multiplied by 6 is 24? ☐

The fifth multiple of 3 is 18.
True or false? _____

3 Here are some clothes for sale. How much does it cost to buy:

8 caps £ ☐

3 caps £ ☐

6 caps £ ☐

4 t-shirts £ ☐

7 t-shirts £ ☐

9 t-shirts £ ☐

How many caps can you buy for £27? ☐

How many t-shirts can you buy for £30? ☐

£3

£6

4 Here are some targets. If an arrow lands in the white ring it scores 3 times the number. If an arrow lands in the blue ring it scores 6 times the number. If an arrow lands on the grey ring it scores 9 times the number.
Complete the score for each target.

$8 \times 3 =$ [ ]

[ ]

[ ]

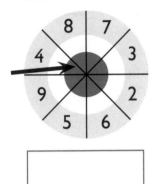

[ ]

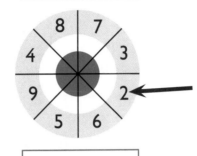

[ ]

[ ]

5 Draw a line to join each multiplication to its answer.

(9 × 3) (5 × 3) (3 × 6) (12 × 6) (4 × 9) (11 × 9)

Parent tip
Use a calculator to go through the three, six and nine times tables with your child.

(15) (99) (36) (27) (18) (72)

6 Write in the missing numbers.

[ ] × 3 = 24   [ ] × 6 = 30   6 × [ ] = 54

5 × [ ] = 15   7 × 6 = [ ]   9 × 3 = [ ]

[ ] × 6 = 54   [ ] × 3 = 33   12 × 9 = [ ]

How much did you do?   **Questions 1-6**

Circle the star to show what you have done.

 Some   Most   All

Eleven times table

The eleven times table tells you how to count in sets of eleven.

1 Shade a path from Start to Finish that only goes through answers in the eleven times table.

Start →

88	11	66	60	23
19	71	44	8	27
34	56	110	15	41
72	39	55	22	77
90	8	101	98	33
17	1	10	84	99

→ Finish

2 Write the number in the smaller square that is multiplied by 11 to give the number in the larger square.

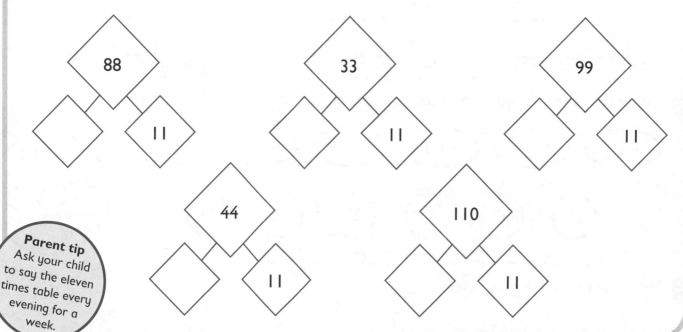

Parent tip
Ask your child to say the eleven times table every evening for a week.

3 Answer these questions.

Multiply 6 by 11. ☐   What is the fifth multiple of eleven? ☐

What do you need to multiply 11 by to get 88? ☐

What is the product of ten and eleven? ☐

A cake costs 11p. What is the cost of 5 cakes? ☐ p

4 See if you can complete the multiplication facts on the race track in less than two minutes. Time yourself!

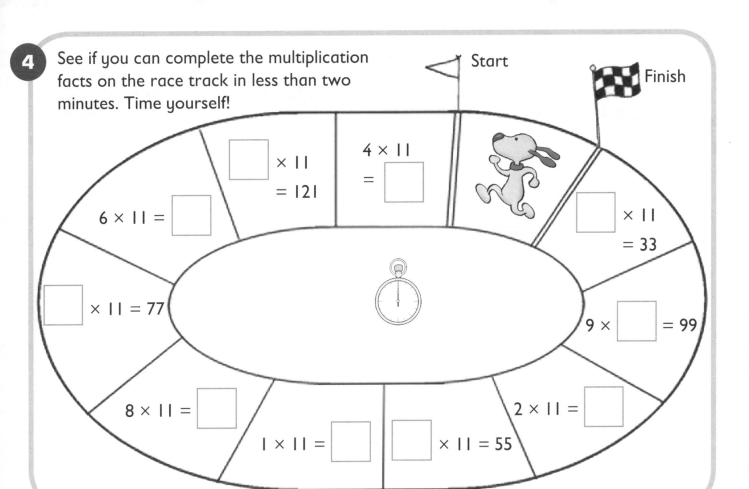

Start

Finish

$\boxed{} \times 11 = 121$

$4 \times 11 = \boxed{}$

$6 \times 11 = \boxed{}$

$\boxed{} \times 11 = 33$

$\boxed{} \times 11 = 77$

$9 \times \boxed{} = 99$

$8 \times 11 = \boxed{}$

$1 \times 11 = \boxed{}$

$\boxed{} \times 11 = 55$

$2 \times 11 = \boxed{}$

5 Complete these multiplications using the eleven times table.

$77 = \boxed{} \times 11$ $44 = \boxed{} \times 11$ $110 = \boxed{} \times 11$

$33 = \boxed{} \times 11$ $99 = \boxed{} \times 11$ $22 = \boxed{} \times 11$

$11 = \boxed{} \times 11$ $88 = \boxed{} \times 11$ $132 = \boxed{} \times 11$

6 Look at the numbers in the oval. Draw boxes around the multiples of 11.

132

35   11   77   67

55   101   21   70   110

66

Twelve times table

The twelve times table tells you how to count in sets of twelve.

1 Every number put into the number machine is multiplied by 12.
Fill in the missing numbers.

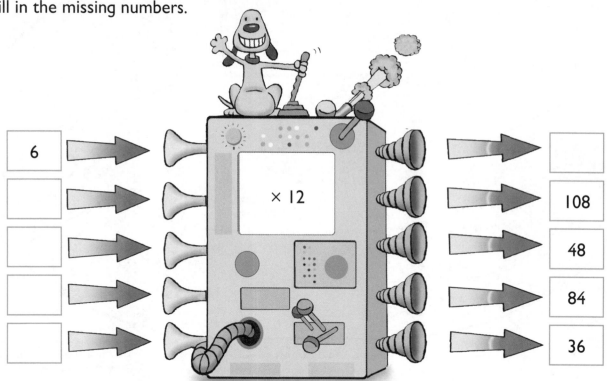

Input	Output
6	
	108
	48
	84
	36

2 Answer these questions.

What is the product of 6 and 12? ☐

What is the eighth multiple of 12? ☐

What do you need to multiply 12 by to get 48? ☐

What is ten times twelve? ☐

How many twelves are in 60? ☐

Multiply 9 by 12. ☐

3 Write the number in the box that multiplies by 12 to give the number in the circle.

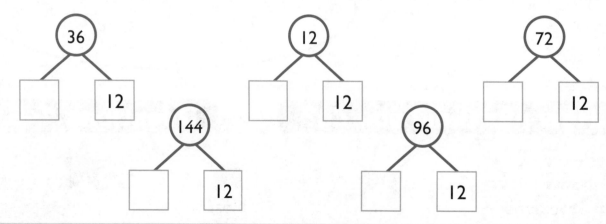

36 → ☐ 12

12 → ☐ 12

72 → ☐ 12

144 → ☐ 12

96 → ☐ 12

4 Complete the sequences by writing the missing multiples of 12.

12   24   ☐   ☐   60   ☐   ☐

144   ☐   120   ☐   ☐   84   ☐

48   ☐   72   ☐   ☐   108   ☐

5 The teacher has written four multiplications on each whiteboard.
Put a tick next to those with the correct answer.   ✔
Put a cross next to those with the wrong answer.   ✘

$5 \times 12 = 60$

$9 \times 12 = 108$

$3 \times 12 = 48$

$10 \times 12 = 96$

$8 \times 12 = 96$

$4 \times 12 = 36$

$2 \times 12 = 24$

$7 \times 12 = 84$

6 In each line, circle the answer that matches the multiplication in the box.

6×12	84	72	60	48
9×12	90	96	108	120
4×12	58	48	36	54
11×12	96	108	132	92

Parent tip
Use sticky notes
to create a twelve
times table trail
around the
house.

How much did you do?   **Questions 1–6**

Circle the star
to show what
you have done.

Some

Most

All

Mixed tables

1 Look at the numbers in the box.
Circle in red the multiples of 4.
Circle in green the multiples of 8.
Circle in blue the multiples of 12.

Which numbers have been circled
in red, green and blue?

_____

8		28		48
	16	36	20	
12		24		132

2 Work out the answers to each multiplication.
Use the answers to find the correct colour in
the code key.

Colour the picture.

Code key
12 = red
144 = brown
16 = green
24 = yellow
40 = pink
96 = purple

Parent tip
Try texting
questions on the
four, eight and
twelve times tables
to your child.

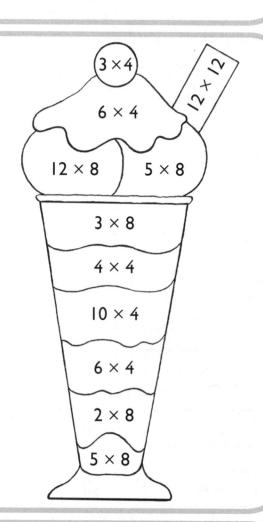

3×4
12×12
6×4
12×8 5×8
3×8
4×4
10×4
6×4
2×8
5×8

3 In each line, circle all the multiplications that match the number in the box.

32	3×12	8×4	9×4	4×8
20	6×4	2×8	5×4	3×8
24	2×12	6×4	3×8	5×4
36	9×4	12×2	4×8	3×12

4 Answer these questions.

Multiply 9 by 4. ☐

What are nine twelves? ☐

What is 8 multiplied by itself? ☐

What is the product of 4 and 12? ☐

What is the eleventh multiple of 8? ☐

The fifth multiple of 4 is 24.
True or false? _____

5 Complete the times table wheels for the four and eight times tables.

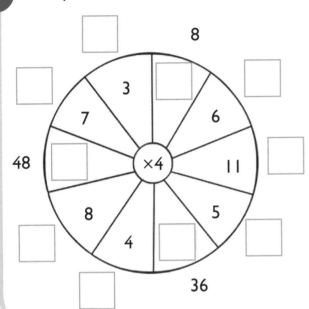

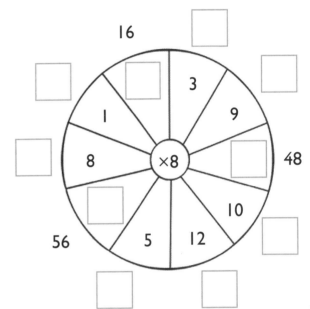

6 Use the four times table facts to work out the answers to the eight times table facts.

$1 \times 4 = 4$

$1 \times 8 = 8$

$3 \times 4 = 12$

$3 \times 8 = $ ☐

$4 \times 4 = 16$

$4 \times 8 = $ ☐

$12 \times 4 = 48$

$12 \times 8 = $ ☐

$8 \times 4 = 32$

$8 \times 8 = $ ☐

$9 \times 4 = 36$

$9 \times 8 = $ ☐

Mixed tables

1 So you think you know the nine times table?
Write out the full table below.

| □ | × | □ | = | □ | | □ | × | □ | = | □ | | □ | × | □ | = | □ |

| □ | × | □ | = | □ | | □ | × | □ | = | □ | | □ | × | □ | = | □ |

| □ | × | □ | = | □ | | □ | × | □ | = | □ | | □ | × | □ | = | □ |

| □ | × | □ | = | □ | | □ | × | □ | = | □ | | □ | × | □ | = | □ |

2 Complete the times table wheels for the nine and twelve times tables.

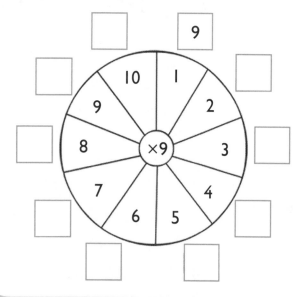

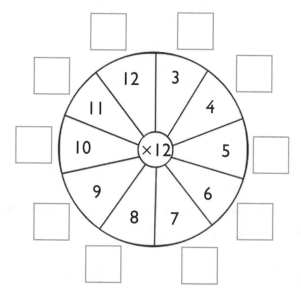

3 So you think you know the eleven times table?
Write out the full table below.

| □ | × | □ | = | □ | | □ | × | □ | = | □ | | □ | × | □ | = | □ |

| □ | × | □ | = | □ | | □ | × | □ | = | □ | | □ | × | □ | = | □ |

| □ | × | □ | = | □ | | □ | × | □ | = | □ | | □ | × | □ | = | □ |

| □ | × | □ | = | □ | | □ | × | □ | = | □ | | □ | × | □ | = | □ |

4 Draw a line to join each multiplication to its answer.

4×9 10×11 4×12 7×9 7×12 9×9 7×11

77 48 81 63 36 110 84

5 Work out each multiplication and write the answer in the grid.
The last digit of each answer is the first digit of the next answer.
The first one has been filled in for you.

1	2 × 9	7	4 × 12
2	7 × 12	8	8 × 11
3	4 × 11	9	9 × 9
4	5 × 9	10	1 × 11
5	5 × 11	11	1 × 12
6	6 × 9		

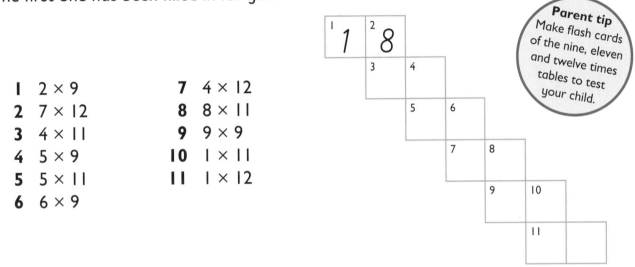

Parent tip
Make flash cards of the nine, eleven and twelve times tables to test your child.

6 So you think you know the twelve times table?
Write out the full table below.

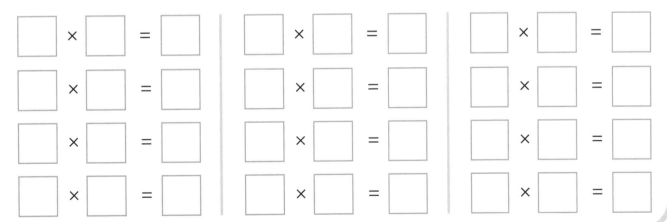

☐ × ☐ = ☐   ☐ × ☐ = ☐   ☐ × ☐ = ☐

☐ × ☐ = ☐   ☐ × ☐ = ☐   ☐ × ☐ = ☐

☐ × ☐ = ☐   ☐ × ☐ = ☐   ☐ × ☐ = ☐

☐ × ☐ = ☐   ☐ × ☐ = ☐   ☐ × ☐ = ☐

How much did you do?   Questions 1–6

Circle the star to show what you have done.

 Some   Most   All

Odd tables

1 Work out the answers across and down to complete the puzzles.

(4) × (3) = ☐   (6) × (9) = ☐

×   ×   ×   ×

(9) × (5) = ☐   (7) × (3) = ☐

=   =   =   =

☐   ☐   ☐   ☐

2 Complete the multiplication grid.

Parent tip
Record mixed tables facts on a media player for your child to listen to and repeat.

×	12	9	7	8	4
3					
7					
5					
9					

3 Here is a machine that sorts numbers. Sort the numbers into multiples of five, seven and nine and write them in the correct bucket. Cross out the numbers as you sort them.

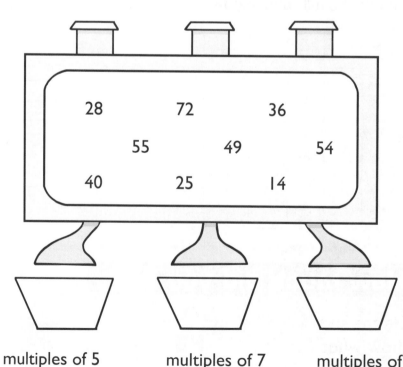

28   72   36
    55   49   54
40   25   14

multiples of 5   multiples of 7   multiples of 9

28

4 An archer fires three arrows. He multiplies the number on the arrow by the score on the target. Work out the score for each arrow. Write the scores in the boxes next to each arrow.

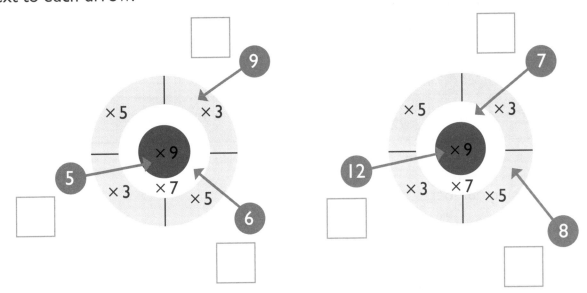

5 Answer these questions.

What are eight sevens? ☐

What is 7 multiplied by 11? ☐

How many nines in 72? ☐

Multiply ten by five. ☐

Find the product of 4 and 3. ☐

Multiply seven by itself. ☐

6 An adult ticket for the cinema costs £8 and a child ticket costs £6.
How much would it cost for:

5 adult tickets £ ☐

7 child tickets £ ☐

9 adult tickets £ ☐

3 child tickets £ ☐

Adult
£8

Child
£6

How much did you do?　　**Questions 1-6**

Circle the star
to show what
you have done.

Some

Most

All

7 Here is part of a number grid. Write a multiplication from the three, five, seven or nine times table for each of the missing numbers. The first one has been done for you.

11	4 × 3	13			16	17		19	
	22	23			26			29	
31	32		34			37	38	39	

8 Fill in the missing numbers.

☐ × 3 = 6   ☐ × 5 = 20   ☐ × 9 = 90

☐ × 7 = 28   ☐ × 3 = 15   ☐ × 7 = 14

☐ × 9 = 54   ☐ × 7 = 56   ☐ × 3 = 36

☐ × 5 = 5   ☐ × 9 = 36   ☐ × 5 = 50

9 Colour the picture using the code key below.

Code key
answers in the 3 times table = brown
answers in the 5 times table = blue
answers in the 7 times table = yellow
answers in the 9 times table = green

Parent tip
Take turns to recite alternate three, five, seven and nine times tables facts with your child.

10 Complete this speed test. Record your score and time taken below the speed test.

$2 \times 5 =$ ▢ $4 \times 7 =$ ▢ $11 \times 7 =$ ▢

$11 \times 3 =$ ▢ $10 \times 7 =$ ▢ $6 \times 3 =$ ▢

$10 \times 9 =$ ▢ $3 \times 9 =$ ▢ $3 \times 7 =$ ▢

$5 \times 9 =$ ▢ $12 \times 5 =$ ▢ $7 \times 5 =$ ▢

$7 \times 7 =$ ▢ $6 \times 9 =$ ▢ $12 \times 7 =$ ▢

$1 \times 5 =$ ▢ $2 \times 9 =$ ▢ $9 \times 5 =$ ▢

$12 \times 9 =$ ▢ $8 \times 5 =$ ▢ $1 \times 9 =$ ▢

$1 \times 3 =$ ▢ $2 \times 3 =$ ▢ $2 \times 7 =$ ▢

$9 \times 3 =$ ▢ $8 \times 3 =$ ▢ $6 \times 7 =$ ▢

$11 \times 5 =$ ▢ $1 \times 7 =$ ▢ $3 \times 5 =$ ▢

$7 \times 9 =$ ▢ $12 \times 3 =$ ▢ $11 \times 9 =$ ▢

$10 \times 5 =$ ▢ $8 \times 9 =$ ▢ $6 \times 5 =$ ▢

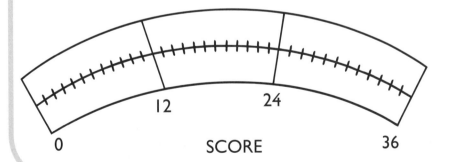

0   12   24   36

SCORE

TIME

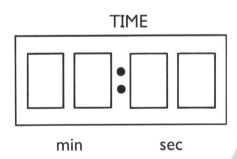

min   sec

Odd tables

Sevens, nines and elevens

1 For each pyramid, work out the answer in each circle.
Colour yellow the circle with the highest answer.
Colour purple the circle with the lowest answer.

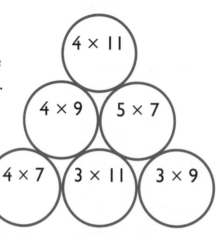

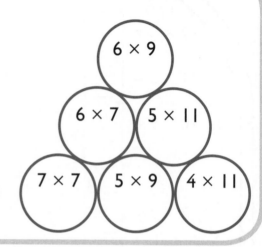

2 Fill in the answers on the multiplication steps.

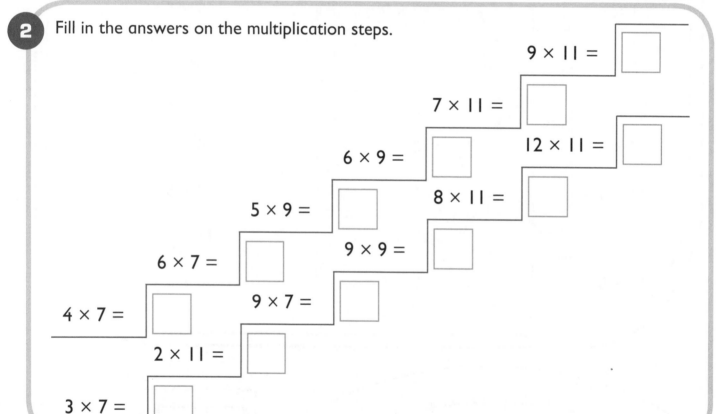

$9 \times 11 = \square$

$7 \times 11 = \square$

$12 \times 11 = \square$

$6 \times 9 = \square$

$8 \times 11 = \square$

$5 \times 9 = \square$

$9 \times 9 = \square$

$6 \times 7 = \square$

$9 \times 7 = \square$

$4 \times 7 = \square$

$2 \times 11 = \square$

$3 \times 7 = \square$

3 Complete the multiplication grids.

×	7	9
2		
4		
6		

×	7	11
1		
5		
8		

×	9	11
3		
7		
10		

4 Find the product of:

3 and 9 ☐   7 and 7 ☐

10 and 11 ☐   12 and 9 ☐

8 and 9 ☐   7 and 11 ☐

Parent tip
Ask your child to write out the full seven, nine and eleven times tables.

5 Here are the ticket prices for entry to a funfair.
How much would it cost to buy tickets for:

Adult	£11
Child under 16	£9
Child under 10	£7

9 adults   £ ☐

4 children under 16   £ ☐

12 children under 10   £ ☐

How many adult tickets can you buy with £33? ☐

How many tickets for children under 16 can you buy with £54? ☐

6 An archer fires three arrows. He multiplies the number on the arrow by the score on the target. Work out the score for each arrow. Write the scores in the boxes next to each arrow.

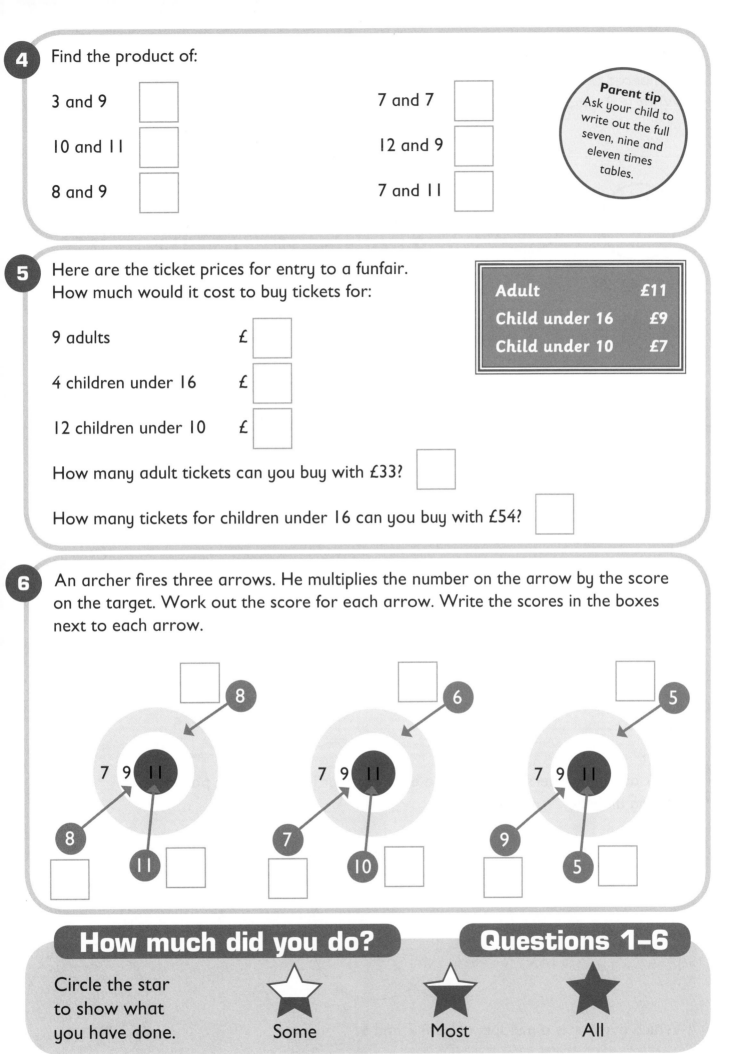

How much did you do?   Questions 1–6

Circle the star to show what you have done.

Some   Most   All

7 Work out the answer to the multiplication in each bubble. Find this answer in the numbered boxes below. Write the letter from that bubble in the space above the box. What is the hidden animal?

_____

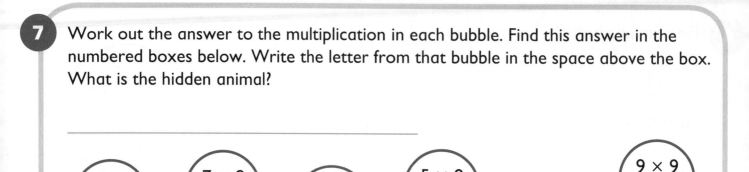

Bubbles:
- 6 × 7 **I**
- 7 × 9 **A**
- 6 × 11 **G**
- 5 × 9 **F**
- 4 × 11 **E**
- 9 × 9 **R**

| 66 | 42 | 81 | 63 | 45 | 45 | 44 |

8 Complete the multiples of seven. Write each digit in a separate box.

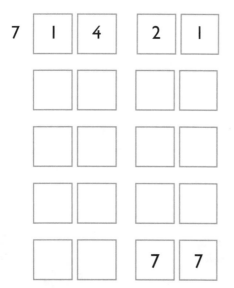

7 | 1 | 4 | | 2 | 1

(empty boxes)

| | 7 | 7

Draw lines to join the last digit of each multiple to make a pattern in the circle.

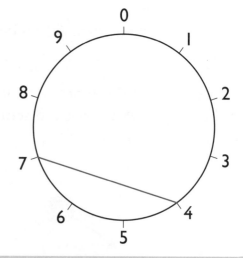

9 Look at the numbers below. Write each number in the correct part of the sorting diagram.

27   21   54   99   49   81   42   36   63   56

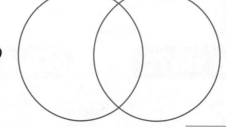

multiples of 9   multiples of 7

Which number is a multiple of both 7 and 9? [ ]

10 Complete this speed test. Record your score and time taken below the speed test.

3 × 11 =	6 × 9 =	12 × 9 =
9 × 7 =	11 × 11 =	4 × 11 =
11 × 9 =	9 × 9 =	4 × 7 =
7 × 11 =	3 × 9 =	10 × 11 =
7 × 7 =	2 × 11 =	6 × 7 =
1 × 11 =	11 × 7 =	6 × 11 =
2 × 7 =	8 × 11 =	2 × 9 =
8 × 9 =	1 × 7 =	7 × 9 =
3 × 7 =	1 × 9 =	12 × 11 =
5 × 11 =	10 × 7 =	5 × 9 =
12 × 7 =	10 × 9 =	8 × 7 =
9 × 11 =	5 × 7 =	4 × 9 =

TIME

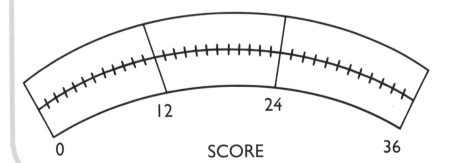

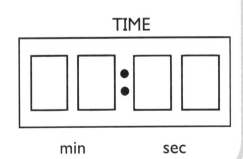

0   SCORE   36   min   sec

Even tables

1 For each triangle, colour red the part with the highest answer. Colour blue the part with the lowest answer.

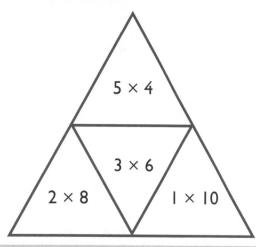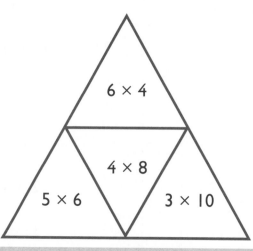

2 Complete the multiplication grids.

×	7	2
8		
4		

×	3	5
8		
10		

×		
6	36	
8		96

3 Complete the multiplication steps.

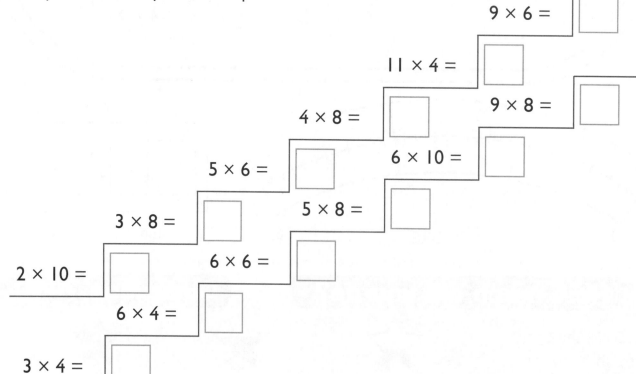

$9 \times 6 =$ ☐

$11 \times 4 =$ ☐

$4 \times 8 =$ ☐

$9 \times 8 =$ ☐

$5 \times 6 =$ ☐

$6 \times 10 =$ ☐

$3 \times 8 =$ ☐

$5 \times 8 =$ ☐

$2 \times 10 =$ ☐

$6 \times 6 =$ ☐

$6 \times 4 =$ ☐

$3 \times 4 =$ ☐

4 Fill in the missing numbers.

☐ × 4 = 12	☐ × 6 = 24	☐ × 8 = 40
☐ × 10 = 60	☐ × 6 = 42	☐ × 4 = 32
☐ × 10 = 120	☐ × 8 = 64	☐ × 10 = 50
☐ × 8 = 88	☐ × 6 = 36	☐ × 4 = 20

5 Work out the answers to each multiplication. Use the answers to find the correct colour in the code key. Colour the picture.

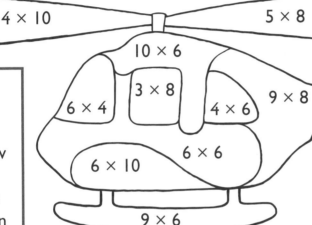

Code key
24 = blue
36 = grey
40 = yellow
54 = black
60 = green
72 = brown

6 Complete the number sequences using multiples of four, six, eight or ten.

18	24	☐	☐	☐	☐
48	40	☐	☐	☐	☐
48	44	☐	☐	☐	☐
☐	☐	40	☐	20	☐

Parent tip
Ask your child to write out the four, six, eight and ten times tables in full.

How much did you do?   Questions 1–6

Circle the star to show what you have done.

 Some   Most   All

7 Work out the answer to the multiplication in each bubble. Find this answer in the numbered boxes below. Write the letter from that bubble in the space above the box. What is the hidden word?

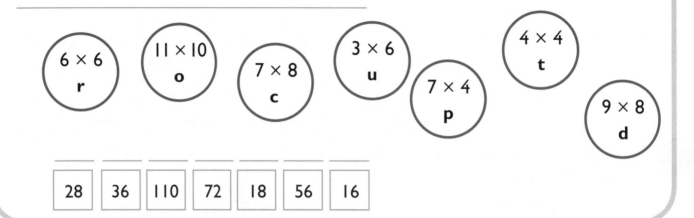

6 × 6
r

11 × 10
o

7 × 8
c

3 × 6
u

7 × 4
p

4 × 4
t

9 × 8
d

| 28 | 36 | 110 | 72 | 18 | 56 | 16 |

8 In each line, circle the multiplication or multiplications that match the number in the box.

40	9 × 4	7 × 6	4 × 10	5 × 8
12	3 × 4	2 × 8	2 × 10	2 × 6
54	7 × 8	6 × 10	9 × 6	6 × 8
24	6 × 4	4 × 6	3 × 8	3 × 10

Parent tip
Ask your child to make a poster of the four, six, eight and ten times tables to stick on the wall.

9 It costs £10 to hire a taxi. The taxi can carry six people and eight bags.

How much would it cost to hire 3 taxis? £ ☐

How many bags can 7 taxis carry? ☐

How many people can 11 taxis carry? ☐

How many wheels are there on 6 taxis? ☐

A group of 24 people needs to hire taxis.

How many taxis will they need? ☐

How much will it cost? £ ☐

10 Complete this speed test. Record your score and time taken below the speed test.

$4 \times 4 =$ ☐ $8 \times 4 =$ ☐ $10 \times 6 =$ ☐

$12 \times 6 =$ ☐ $11 \times 10 =$ ☐ $4 \times 8 =$ ☐

$9 \times 8 =$ ☐ $9 \times 4 =$ ☐ $12 \times 10 =$ ☐

$7 \times 10 =$ ☐ $12 \times 8 =$ ☐ $8 \times 6 =$ ☐

$11 \times 4 =$ ☐ $4 \times 6 =$ ☐ $6 \times 8 =$ ☐

$7 \times 8 =$ ☐ $6 \times 10 =$ ☐ $7 \times 6 =$ ☐

$3 \times 6 =$ ☐ $1 \times 8 =$ ☐ $11 \times 8 =$ ☐

$2 \times 8 =$ ☐ $9 \times 6 =$ ☐ $7 \times 4 =$ ☐

$2 \times 6 =$ ☐ $10 \times 8 =$ ☐ $12 \times 4 =$ ☐

$3 \times 8 =$ ☐ $11 \times 6 =$ ☐ $5 \times 4 =$ ☐

$6 \times 6 =$ ☐ $10 \times 4 =$ ☐ $5 \times 8 =$ ☐

$9 \times 10 =$ ☐ $8 \times 8 =$ ☐ $5 \times 6 =$ ☐

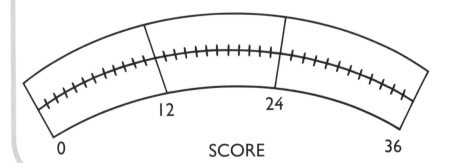

TIME

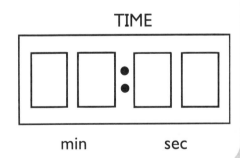

0   12   24   36   min   sec

SCORE

Even tables

Sixes, eights and twelves

1 Complete the puzzle by finding the answers to the multiplications.

Across	Down
2 2 × 6	**1** 9 × 8
3 9 × 12	**2** 10 × 12
5 6 × 6	**3** 2 × 8
6 6 × 8	**4** 7 × 12
	5 4 × 8
	7 11 × 8

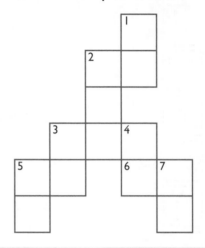

2 Complete the first six multiples of six and eight. Write each digit in a separate box.

6 | 1 | 2 | | | | | | | | | | |

8 | | | | | | | | | | | | |

Draw lines to join the last digit of each multiple to make patterns in the circles.

Sixes

Eights

3 Complete these times tables facts.

☐ × 6 = 18   ☐ × 8 = 24   ☐ × 12 = 132

☐ × 8 = 56   ☐ × 12 = 96   ☐ × 6 = 42

☐ × 12 = 12   ☐ × 6 = 30   ☐ × 8 = 64

4 Here is a number grid. Shade a path from Start to Finish that only goes through multiples of six, eight or twelve.

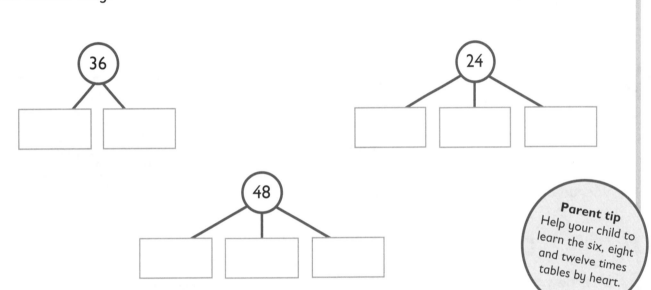

2	38	17	22	7	9	96	→ Finish
7	14	26	19	36	16	84	
34	18	72	60	24	35	11	
48	42	37	62	79	5	13	
54	9	15	73	77	25	31	
12	20	3	49	85	4	1	

Start →

5 For each number, write different multiplication facts from the six, eight and twelve times tables only.

36

24

48

Parent tip
Help your child to learn the six, eight and twelve times tables by heart.

6 Answer these questions.

What is the product of 9 and 8?

What is the eighth multiple of 12?

What do you need to multiply 6 by to get 72?

Which number multiplied by 12 is 84?

How much did you do?   Questions 1–6

Circle the star to show what you have done.

 Some

 Most

 All

7 Use the six, eight and twelve times tables to fill in the missing multiplications and answers in the bricks and make the walls match. The top pair of bricks has been done for you.

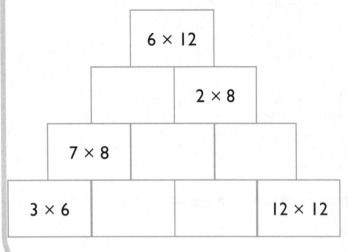
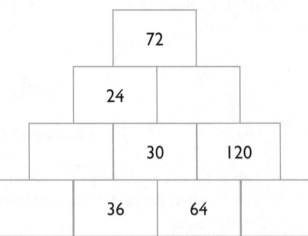

8 Eggs are packed in boxes of different sizes.
How many eggs are there in:

Small	6 eggs
Medium	8 eggs
Large	12 eggs

8 small boxes ☐   5 medium boxes ☐

9 large boxes ☐   11 small boxes ☐

7 medium boxes ☐   3 large boxes ☐

List the ways in which 48 eggs can be packed into boxes of the same size.

_____

9 Write in the multiples of six, eight and twelve to complete the snakes.

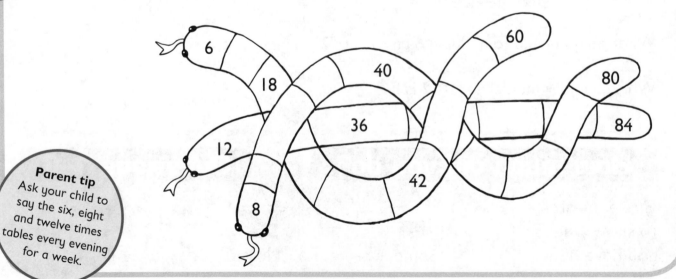

Parent tip
Ask your child to say the six, eight and twelve times tables every evening for a week.

10 Complete this speed test. Record your score and time taken below the speed test.

10 × 6 =	3 × 8 =	6 × 12 =
11 × 12 =	5 × 12 =	4 × 8 =
5 × 8 =	3 × 12 =	10 × 12 =
4 × 12 =	11 × 6 =	6 × 8 =
7 × 8 =	7 × 12 =	2 × 12 =
1 × 12 =	9 × 8 =	3 × 6 =
2 × 8 =	5 × 6 =	8 × 12 =
9 × 12 =	8 × 8 =	12 × 6 =
6 × 6 =	4 × 6 =	1 × 8 =
12 × 8 =	2 × 6 =	1 × 6 =
9 × 6 =	11 × 8 =	10 × 8 =
8 × 6 =	7 × 6 =	12 × 12 =

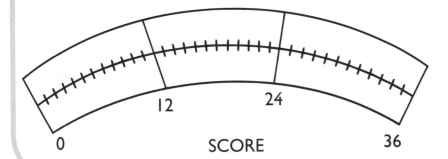

0   12   24   36

SCORE

TIME

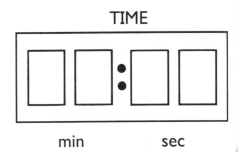

min   sec

Mixed tables

1 This is a recipe to make an ice cream sundae for one person.
Write what you would need to make ice cream sundaes for:

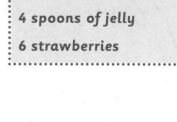

3 scoops of ice cream

4 spoons of jelly

6 strawberries

6 people

☐ scoops of ice cream

☐ spoons of jelly

☐ strawberries

7 people

☐ scoops of ice cream

☐ spoons of jelly

☐ strawberries

2 Choose the correct answer for each multiplication. Colour the letter next to that answer. The letters you have **not** coloured spell out a number.

$4 \times 6 = 24$ ☐ t or 27 ☐ s

$6 \times 9 = 56$ ☐ i or 54 ☐ w

$8 \times 8 = 72$ ☐ x or 64 ☐ a

$4 \times 7 = 28$ ☐ s or 30 ☐ t

$5 \times 9 = 40$ ☐ e or 45 ☐ l

$6 \times 6 = 36$ ☐ i or 35 ☐ e

$12 \times 9 = 64$ ☐ n or 108 ☐ t

Parent tip
Quiz your child once a week on the six, seven, eight and nine times tables.

What is the number? _____

3 Answer these questions.

What is the ninth multiple of nine? ☐

What are four nines? ☐

How many eights in 88? ☐

Multiply 9 by eight. ☐

What number multiplied by 7 is 63? ☐

The fifth multiple of six is 30. True or false? _____

Count on or back to complete each number sequence.

27   36   [ ]   [ ]   63   [ ]   [ ]

49   42   [ ]   [ ]   [ ]   [ ]   7

32   40   [ ]   [ ]   [ ]   [ ]   80

36   [ ]   [ ]   [ ]   60   [ ]   [ ]

---

5 Here are the ticket prices for some attractions.

| Castle | £6 | Funfair | £8 |
| Museum | £7 | Zoo | £9 |

How much would it cost to buy:

Nine funfair tickets   £ [ ]   Six tickets for the castle   £ [ ]

Three museum tickets   £ [ ]   Eight tickets for the zoo   £ [ ]

How many zoo tickets can you buy with £54?   [ ]

How many museum tickets can you buy with £84?   [ ]

---

6 Look at the numbers in the box.
Circle red the multiples of 6.
Circle green the multiples of 7.
Circle blue the multiples of 9.
Circle black the multiples of 8.

12   99   40
    30   64
42   14
    56   63

Which number has been circled in green and black?   [ ]

Which number has been circled in green and blue?   [ ]

Which number has been circled in green and red?   [ ]

How much did you do?   Questions 1–6

Circle the star
to show what
you have done.   ☆   ★   ★
                    Some   Most   All

7 Two people are playing times tables bingo. Here are the tables that have been called.

5×6 6×7 7×9 6×9 9×8 8×7 3×9

Player A

30	42	27
54	72	56

Player B

42	54	72
35	50	63

The player that has the most answers is the winner. Shade the answers on each player's bingo card that match the multiplications.

Who won, Player A or Player B? _____

8 Draw lines to match each multiplication to its answer.

9×6 7×7 9×9 6×8 7×11 3×6

81   18   49   77   54   48

9 Find the right route. You can only go along roads with numbers that are answers in the six, seven, eight and nine times tables.

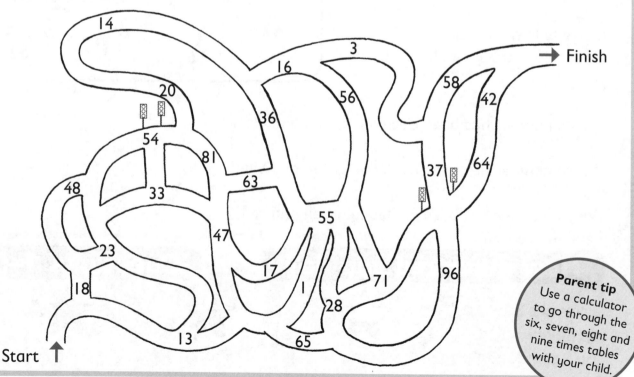

Parent tip
Use a calculator to go through the six, seven, eight and nine times tables with your child.

10 Complete this speed test. Record your score and time taken below the speed test.

$4 \times 9 =$ ☐ $12 \times 7 =$ ☐ $10 \times 6 =$ ☐

$7 \times 8 =$ ☐ $8 \times 9 =$ ☐ $4 \times 8 =$ ☐

$7 \times 7 =$ ☐ $9 \times 9 =$ ☐ $11 \times 9 =$ ☐

$6 \times 9 =$ ☐ $8 \times 7 =$ ☐ $8 \times 6 =$ ☐

$3 \times 6 =$ ☐ $4 \times 7 =$ ☐ $6 \times 8 =$ ☐

$11 \times 7 =$ ☐ $11 \times 6 =$ ☐ $7 \times 6 =$ ☐

$2 \times 8 =$ ☐ $1 \times 8 =$ ☐ $7 \times 9 =$ ☐

$5 \times 9 =$ ☐ $9 \times 6 =$ ☐ $9 \times 8 =$ ☐

$3 \times 8 =$ ☐ $10 \times 8 =$ ☐ $12 \times 8 =$ ☐

$12 \times 9 =$ ☐ $10 \times 9 =$ ☐ $8 \times 8 =$ ☐

$6 \times 6 =$ ☐ $12 \times 6 =$ ☐ $11 \times 8 =$ ☐

$10 \times 7 =$ ☐ $5 \times 8 =$ ☐ $5 \times 6 =$ ☐

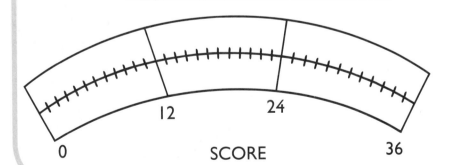

TIME

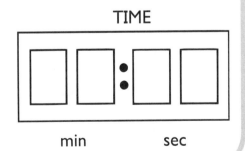

12   24

0   SCORE   36   min   sec

Mixed tables

1 For each hexagon, colour red the triangle with the highest answer. Colour blue the triangle with the lowest answer.

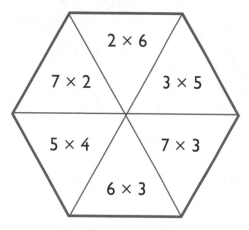

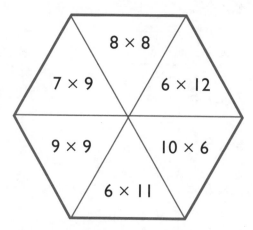

2 Draw lines to match each multiplication to the correct answer.

9×3 7×11 6×4 7×7 9×8 6×2 8×12

24   49   77   12   27   96   72

3 Two numbers that multiply to give another number are called a factor pair.
For example, 5 and 6 and 10 and 3 are both factor pairs of 30.
Complete the factor pairs for the number in the middle.

Parent tip
Use sticky notes to create a mixed tables trail around the house.

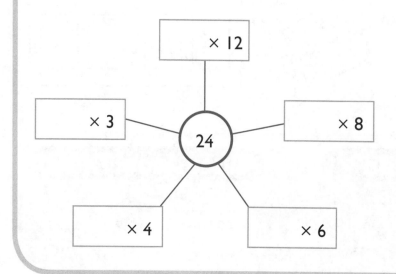

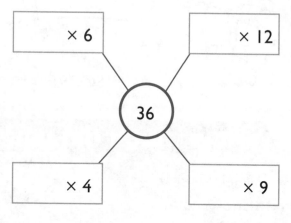

Complete the multiplication grids.

×	7	9	4
4			
6			
7			

×	8	6	3
8			
3			
12			

×	4	10	
	36		
11			55
		20	

---

5 Answer these questions.

What are six nines? ☐

What is four multiplied by two? ☐

What is 8 times 7? ☐

What is the product of 9 and 3? ☐

What is the third multiple of 12? ☐

Which number multiplied by 8 is 48? ☐

---

6 Multiply the number on the arrow by the score on the target. Work out the score for each arrow. Write the score in the box next to each arrow.

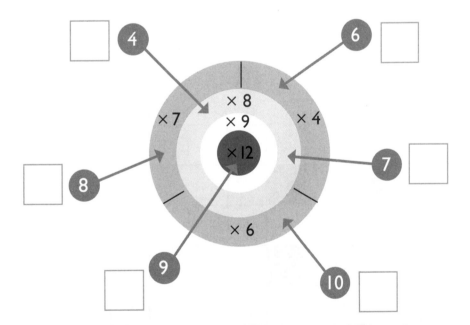

How much did you do?　　　**Questions 1–6**

Circle the star to show what you have done.

☆ Some　　　★ Most　　　★ All

7 Choose two different numbers from the box. Write out the numbers as a multiplication on a piece of paper and then work out the answer. Make as many multiplications as you can.

> 5   7
>   8   4
> 2   9   6

8 Fill in the missing numbers.

☐ × 2 = 18

☐ × 5 = 45

☐ × 8 = 72

☐ × 10 = 50

☐ × 3 = 24

☐ × 6 = 18

☐ × 9 = 36

☐ × 11 = 99

☐ × 4 = 36

☐ × 7 = 56

☐ × 9 = 9

☐ × 12 = 24

9 Complete each sequence of multiples to solve the number puzzle.

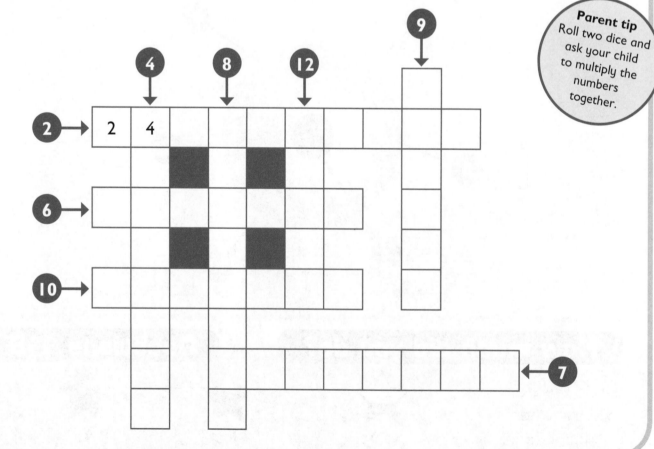

Parent tip
Roll two dice and ask your child to multiply the numbers together.

10 In each line, draw boxes round the multiplications that match the number in the circle.

(72)	8 × 9	6 × 12	9 × 7	8 × 8
(45)	4 × 11	5 × 9	7 × 6	9 × 5
(60)	5 × 12	7 × 9	7 × 8	10 × 6
(48)	7 × 7	8 × 6	4 × 12	5 × 9

11 Work out the multiplications across and down to complete the puzzles.

⑧ × ⑨ = ☐   ⑥ × ⑦ = ☐
×   ×   ×   ×
④ × ⑥ = ☐   ⑧ × ⑦ = ☐
=   =   =   =
☐   ☐   ☐   ☐

12 Use the odd number times tables to fill in the missing multiplications and answers in the bricks and make the walls match. The top pair of bricks has been done for you.

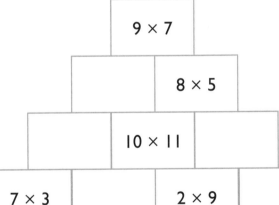

Wall 1:
9 × 7
☐ | 8 × 5
☐ | 10 × 11 | ☐
7 × 3 | ☐ | 2 × 9 | ☐

Wall 2:
63
☐ | 25
☐ | 42 | ☐ | 27
☐ | 72 | ☐ | 55

13 Complete the puzzle by finding the answers to the multiplications.

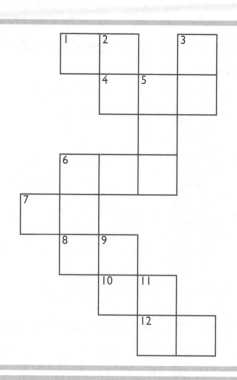

Across
1. 9×8
4. 10×11
6. 10×12
7. 6×10
8. 9×9
10. 8×8
12. 8×6

Down
2. 3×7
3. 4×5
5. 10×10
6. 9×12
9. 4×4
11. 4×11

14 Here are some multiplications. Some are correct and some are not.
Put a tick next to those with the correct answer. ✔
Put a cross next to those with the wrong answer. ✘

$8 \times 7 = 56$ ☐

$7 \times 6 = 48$ ☐

$8 \times 9 = 74$ ☐

$6 \times 12 = 72$ ☐

$7 \times 3 = 24$ ☐

$8 \times 4 = 32$ ☐

$5 \times 8 = 42$ ☐

$9 \times 11 = 99$ ☐

Parent tip
Use the progress certificate at the back of this book to make a reward chart for your child.

15 Fill in the missing numbers in the number machine.

☐ → | ☐ → | 48

☐ → | ☐ → | 108

☐ → | × 12 | → | 24

☐ → | ☐ → | 96

☐ → | ☐ → | 36

Complete the ultimate tables test. Record your score and time below.

3 × 2 =	4 × 12 =	7 × 5 =
6 × 3 =	2 × 12 =	7 × 12 =
7 × 2 =	5 × 3 =	10 × 2 =
9 × 4 =	9 × 2 =	4 × 8 =
5 × 4 =	5 × 11 =	1 × 11 =
3 × 4 =	2 × 7 =	2 × 9 =
5 × 6 =	7 × 3 =	9 × 11 =
8 × 6 =	9 × 10 =	10 × 9 =
6 × 6 =	6 × 9 =	6 × 10 =
12 × 11 =	1 × 4 =	4 × 2 =
9 × 5 =	8 × 9 =	10 × 5 =
9 × 7 =	8 × 7 =	2 × 11 =
4 × 9 =	6 × 7 =	7 × 4 =
8 × 10 =	12 × 12 =	9 × 3 =
9 × 8 =	3 × 5 =	6 × 2 =
9 × 12 =	3 × 3 =	4 × 7 =

SCORE

TIME

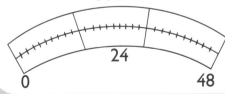

24

0   48

□□ : □□

min   sec

41–48   Outstanding!
33–40   Very good
25–32   Getting there
24 or less   Have another go!

How much did you do?

Questions 13–16

Circle the star
to show what
you have done.

Some

Most

All

Answers

Six times table

Page 4

1 Circle 36, 12, 18, 66, 42

2 brilliant!

3 £12, £42, £30, £60, £72, £36, 3, 8

Page 5

4 3×6; 7×6; 4×6; 8×6

5 $3 \times 6 = 18$; $2 \times 6 = 12$; $5 \times 6 = 30$

6 12, 24, 36, 42, 48; 42, 30, 24, 12, 6; 24, 42, 48, 54, 60; 60, 54, 48, 42, 30

Seven times table

Page 6

1 3, 10, 42, 35, 4, 11, 7, 9, 49, 56

2 $1 \times 7 = 7$; $2 \times 7 = 14$; $5 \times 7 = 35$; $6 \times 7 = 42$; $4 \times 7 = 28$

3 14, 42, 28, 84

Page 7

4 21, 56, 63, 11, 4

5 35; 84; 63; 4; 42; 7, 14, 21

6 Colour 35, 7, 70, 21, 49, 42, 28, 56, 63, 14; the letter T

Eight times table

Page 8

1 24; $6 \times 8 = 48$; $9 \times 8 = 72$; $2 \times 8 = 16$

2 ✗, ✔, ✔, ✗, ✔, ✔, ✗, ✔

3 Start, 24, 16, 8, 56, 80, 72, 32, 64, 40, 96, Finish

Page 9

4 $2 \times 8 = 16$; $3 \times 8 = 24$; $6 \times 8 = 48$; $5 \times 8 = 40$; $7 \times 8 = 56$

5 Colour 8, 64, 48, 80, 40, 72, 32, 88; the letter X

6 48, 56, 12, 64, 48, 4

Mixed tables (threes and sixes)

Page 10

1 24, 24, 6, 54, 12, 30, 18, 21, 9, 36, 15, 30, 18, 42, 66, 27, 48, 12

2 12, 18, 30, 36, 42; 36, 24, 18, 12, 6; 15, 18, 24, 27, 30

3 $\times 6 - 6$, 60, 18, 72, 54, 42; $\times 3 - 3$, 30, 9, 36, 27, 21

Page 11

4 $\times 3 - 6$, 12, 15, 21, 24, 27, 30, 33; $\times 6 - 6$, 12, 18, 30, 42, 48, 54, 60

5 18, 24, 36, 48, 54

6 Start, 12, 15, 36, 18, 21, 42, 27, 60, 6, 3, 48, Finish

Mixed tables (fours and eights)

Page 12

1 8, 24, 56, 64, 40, 4, 16, 72, 16, 48, 24, 36, 20, 40, 88, 12

2 $3 \times 4 = 12$; $6 \times 8 = 48$; $4 \times 4 = 16$; $2 \times 8 = 16$; $9 \times 4 = 36$; $7 \times 4 = 28$

3 6×4 and 24; 4×4 and 16; 12×4 and 48; 8×8 and 64; 5×8 and 40; 5×4 and 20

Page 13

4 Never give up!

5 Circle 32, 16, 8, 40

6 £32, £44, £20, £56, £28, £64

Mixed tables (sixes, sevens and eights)

Page 14

1 $9 \times 7 = 63$; $9 \times 6 = 54$ and $3 \times 6 = 18$; $4 \times 8 = 32$ and $11 \times 8 = 88$

2 Red – 54, 30, 12;
blue – 35, 77, 21, 14;
green – 32, 40, 64

3 30, 48, 63, 64, 56, 72

Page 15

4 Top row – 3, 6; ×7 – 35, 56, 84;
×8 – 40, 64, 96; ×6 – 30, 48, 72

5 A: $8 \times 6 = 48$, B: $7 \times 7 = 49$,
C: $6 \times 6 = 36$, D: $6 \times 7 = 42$,
E: $5 \times 8 = 40$, F: $8 \times 8 = 64$

6 24, 7, 8, 30, 2, 6, 18, 60, 40, 8, 7, 6, 9, 7, 66

Nine times table

Page 16

1 Circle 45, 36, 9, 81, 108

2 $1 \times 9 = 9$; $5 \times 9 = 45$; $3 \times 9 = 27$;
$7 \times 9 = 63$; $4 \times 9 = 36$

3 90

Page 17

4 2×9 and 18; 6×9 and 54;
4×9 and 36; 9×9 and 81;
1×9 and 9; 7×9 and 63

5 2, 11, 5, 8, 7

6 27 and 72; 18 and 81; 54 and 45; 63 and 36; the digits are reversed

Mixed tables (threes, sixes and nines)

Page 18

1 $10 \times 3 = 30$, $5 \times 6 = 30$; $6 \times 3 = 18$,
$3 \times 6 = 18$, $2 \times 9 = 18$; $12 \times 3 = 36$,
$6 \times 6 = 36$, $4 \times 9 = 36$

2 36, 45, 9, 4, 66, false

3 £24, £24, £9, £42, £18, £54, 9, 5

Page 19

4 $8 \times 3 = 24$; $7 \times 6 = 42$; $6 \times 9 = 54$;
$4 \times 6 = 24$; $2 \times 9 = 18$; $9 \times 6 = 54$

5 9×3 and 27; 5×3 and 15;
3×6 and 18; 12×6 and 72;
4×9 and 36; 11×9 and 99

6 8, 5, 9, 3, 42, 27, 9, 11, 108

Eleven times table

Page 20

1 Start, 88, 11, 66, 44, 110, 55, 22, 77, 33, 99, Finish

2 8, 3, 9, 4, 10

3 66, 55, 8, 110, 55p

Page 21

4 44, 11, 66, 7, 88, 11, 5, 22, 11, 3

5 7, 4, 10, 3, 9, 2, 1, 8, 12

6 132, 11, 77, 55, 110, 66

Twelve times table

Page 22

1 72, 9, 4, 7, 3

2 72, 120, 96, 5, 4, 108

3 3, 1, 6, 12, 8

Page 23

4 36, 48, 72, 84; 132, 108, 96, 72;
60, 84, 96, 120

5 ✔, ✔, ✗, ✗, ✔, ✗, ✔, ✔

6 72, 108, 48, 132

Mixed tables (fours, eights and twelves)

Page 24

1. Circle red 8, 28, 48, 16, 36, 20, 12, 24;
circle green 8, 48, 16, 24;
circle blue 48, 36, 12, 24, 132;
all circle colours 48 and 24

2. 3×4 = red; 12×12 = brown;
4×4 and 2×8 = green;
3×8 and 6×4 = yellow;
5×8 and 10×4 = pink;
12×8 = purple

3. $32 = 8 \times 4$ and 4×8; $20 = 5 \times 4$;
$24 = 2 \times 12$, 6×4, 3×8;
$36 = 9 \times 4$ and 3×12

Page 25

4. 36, 48, 108, 88, 64, false

5. (Clockwise from top) $\times 4$ – 2, 24, 44, 20, 9, 16, 32, 12, 28, 12; $\times 8$ – 24, 72, 6, 80, 96, 40, 7, 64, 8, 2

6. 24, 32, 96, 64, 72

Mixed tables (nines, elevens and twelves)

Page 26

1. See page 62 for the full nine times table

2. (Clockwise from the top) $\times 9$ – 18, 27, 36, 45, 54, 63, 72, 81, 90;
$\times 12$ – 36, 48, 60, 72, 84, 96, 108, 120, 132, 144

3. See page 62 for the full eleven times table

Page 27

4. 4×9 and 36; 10×11 and 110;
4×12 and 48; 7×9 and 63; 7×12 and 84; 9×9 and 81; 7×11 and 77

5. 18, 84, 44, 45, 55, 54, 48, 88, 81, 11, 12

6. See page 62 for the full twelve times table

Odd tables (threes, fives, sevens and nines)

Page 28

1. Across 12 and 45, down 36 and 15;
across 54 and 21, down 42 and 27

2. $\times 3$ – 36, 27, 21, 24, 12;
$\times 7$ – 84, 63, 49, 56, 28;
$\times 5$ – 60, 45, 35, 40, 20;
$\times 9$ – 108, 81, 63, 72, 36

3. Multiples of 5 – 55, 40, 25;
multiples of 7 – 28, 49, 14;
multiples of 9 – 72, 36, 54

Page 29

4. (Clockwise from top) 27, 42, 45; 49, 40, 108

5. 56, 50, 77, 12, 8, 49

6. £40, £42, £72, £18

Page 30

7. 2×7, 5×3 or 3×5, 6×3 or 2×9, 4×5; 7×3 or 3×7, 8×3, 5×5, 9×3 or 3×9, 4×7, 10×3 or 6×5; 11×3, 7×5 or 5×7, 4×9 or 12×3, 8×5

8. 2, 4, 10, 4, 5, 2, 6, 8, 12, 1, 4, 10

9. Brown – 12, 6, 3, 24;
blue – 25, 5, 50, 10, 40, 20;
yellow – 49, 70, 28, 14, 56;
green – 72, 81, 99, 108, 54

Page 31

10. 10, 28, 77, 33, 70, 18, 90, 27, 21, 45, 60, 35, 49, 54, 84, 5, 18, 45, 108, 40, 9, 3, 6, 14, 27, 24, 42, 55, 7, 15, 63, 36, 99, 50, 72, 30

Odd tables (sevens, nines and elevens)

Page 32

1 4×11 – yellow, 3×9 – purple; 5×11 – yellow, 6×7 – purple

2 28, 42, 45, 54, 77, 99; 21, 22, 63, 81, 88, 132

3 First grid $\times 7$ – 14, 28, 42; $\times 9$ – 18, 36, 54; second grid $\times 7$ – 7, 35, 56; $\times 11$ – 11, 55, 88; third grid $\times 9$ – 27, 63, 90; $\times 11$ – 33, 77, 110

Page 33

4 27, 49, 110, 108, 72, 77

5 £99, £36, £84, 3, 6

6 (Clockwise from top) 56, 121, 72; 42, 110, 63; 35, 55, 81

Page 34

7 Giraffe

8 28, 35, 42, 49, 56, 63, 70
Lines should be drawn from 7 to every number on the circle.

9 Multiples of 9 – 27, 54, 99, 81, 36, 63; multiples of 7 – 21, 49, 42, 56, 63; 63 multiple of both 7 and 9 – 63

Page 35

10 33, 54, 108, 63, 121, 44, 99, 81, 28, 77, 27, 110, 49, 22, 42, 11, 77, 66, 14, 88, 18, 72, 7, 63, 21, 9, 132, 55, 70, 45, 84, 90, 56, 99, 35, 36

Even tables (fours, sixes, eights and tens)

Page 36

1 5×4 – red, 1×10 – blue; 4×8 – red, 6×4 – blue

2 First grid $\times 8$ – 56, 16; $\times 4$ – 28, 8; second grid $\times 8$ – 24, 40; $\times 10$ – 30, 50; third grid top row 6, 12; $\times 6$ – 72; $\times 8$ – 48

3 20, 24, 30, 32, 44, 54; 12, 24, 36, 40, 60, 72

Page 37

4 3, 4, 5, 6, 7, 8, 12, 8, 5, 11, 6, 5

5 Blue – 6×4, 3×8, 4×6; grey – 9×4, 6×6; yellow – 4×10, 5×8, 10×4, 5×8; black – 9×6; green – 10×6, 6×10; brown – 9×8

6 30, 36, 42, 48; 32, 24, 16, 8; 40, 36, 32, 28; 60, 50, 30, 10

Page 38

7 product

8 4×10 and 5×8; 3×4 and 2×6; 9×6; 6×4, 4×6 and 3×8

9 £30, 56, 66, 24, 4, £40

Page 39

10 16, 32, 60, 72, 110, 32, 72, 36, 120, 70, 96, 48, 44, 24, 48, 56, 60, 42, 18, 8, 88, 16, 54, 28, 12, 80, 48, 24, 66, 20, 36, 40, 40, 90, 64, 30

Even tables (sixes, eights and twelves)

Page 40

1 Across – (2) 12, (3) 108, (5) 36, (6) 48; down – (1) 72, (2) 120, (3) 16, (4) 84, (5) 32, (7) 88

2 18, 24, 30, 36; 16, 24, 32, 40, 48

Sixes circle – lines drawn from 6 to 0, 2, 4, 8

Eights circle – lines drawn from 8 to 0, 2, 4, 6

3 3, 3, 11, 7, 8, 7, 1, 5, 8

Page 41

4 Start, 12, 54, 48, 42, 18, 72, 60, 24, 36, 16, 84, 96, Finish

5 6 × 6, 3 × 12; 4 × 6, 3 × 8, 2 × 12; 8 × 6, 6 × 8, 4 × 12

6 72, 96, 12, 7

Page 42

7 First wall (from top) – 4 × 6 or 3 × 8 or 2 × 12, 5 × 6, 10 × 12, 6 × 6 or 3 × 12, 8 × 8; second wall (from top) – 16, 56, 18, 144

8 48, 40, 108, 66, 56, 36; 8 small boxes, 6 medium boxes and 4 large boxes

9 6 – 12, 24, 30, 36, 48, 54; 8 – 16, 24, 32, 48, 56, 64, 72; 12 – 24, 48, 60, 72

Page 43

10 60, 24, 72, 132, 60, 32, 40, 36, 120, 48, 66, 48, 56, 84, 24, 12, 72, 18, 16, 30, 96, 108, 64, 72, 36, 24, 8, 96, 12, 6, 54, 88, 80, 48, 42, 144

Mixed tables (sixes, sevens, eights and nines)

Page 44

1 6 people – 18, 24, 36; 7 people – 21, 28, 42

2 Shade t, w, a, s, l, i, t; sixteen

3 81, 36, 11, 72, 9, true

Page 45

4 45, 54, 72, 81; 35, 28, 21, 14; 48, 56, 64, 72; 42, 48, 54, 66, 72

5 £72, £36, £21, £72, 6, 12

6 Circle red – 12, 30, 42; circle green – 42, 14, 56, 63; circle blue – 99, 63; circle black – 40, 64, 56; 56, 63, 42

Page 46

7 Player A shade 30, 42, 27, 54, 72, 56; Player B shade 42, 54, 72, 63; Player A won

8 9 × 6 and 54; 7 × 7 and 49; 9 × 9 and 81; 6 × 8 and 48; 7 × 11 and 77; 3 × 6 and 18

9 Start, 18, 48, 54, 81, 63, 36, 16, 56, 28, 96, 64, 42, Finish

Page 47

10 36, 84, 60, 56, 72, 32, 49, 81, 99, 54, 56, 48, 18, 28, 48, 77, 66, 42, 16, 8, 63, 45, 54, 72, 24, 80, 96, 108, 90, 64, 36, 72, 88, 70, 40, 30

Mixed tables (twos to twelves)

Page 48

1 7 × 3 – red, 2 × 6 – blue; 9 × 9 – red, 10 × 6 – blue

2 9 × 3 and 27; 7 × 11 and 77; 6 × 4 and 24; 7 × 7 and 49; 9 × 8 and 72; 6 × 2 and 12; 8 × 12 and 96

3 (Clockwise from top) 2 × 12, 3 × 8, 4 × 6, 6 × 4, 8 × 3; 3 × 12, 4 × 9, 9 × 4, 6 × 6

Page 49

4 First grid ×4 – 28, 36, 16; ×6 – 42, 54, 24; ×7 – 49, 63, 28; second grid ×8 – 64, 48, 24; ×3 – 24, 18, 9; ×12 – 96, 72, 36; third grid top row – 5; ×9 – 90, 45; ×11 – 44, 110; ×2 – 8, 10

5 54, 8, 56, 27, 36, 6

6 (Clockwise from top) 24, 56, 60, 108, 56, 32

Page 50

7 42 different facts are possible

8 9, 8, 9, 9, 3, 8, 9, 4, 1, 5, 9, 2

9 (2) 6, 8, 10, 12, 14, 16, 18, 20;
(4) 8, 12, 16, 20, 24, 28, 32;
(6) 6, 12, 18, 24, 30, 36, 42;
(7) 7, 14, 21, 28, 35, 42, 49, 56;
(8) 8, 16, 24, 32, 40, 48, 56, 64;
(9) 9, 18, 27, 36, 45, 54;
(10) 10, 20, 30, 40, 50, 60, 70;
(12) 12, 24, 36, 48, 60

Page 51

10 8×9 and 6×12; 5×9 and 9×5;
5×12 and 10×6; 8×6 and 4×12

11 Across 72 and 24, down 32 and 54;
across 42 and 56, down 48 and 49

12 First wall (from top) – 5×5, 6×7,
9×3 or 3×9, 8×9, 11×5 or 5×11;
second wall (from top) – 40, 110, 21, 18

Page 52

13 Across – (1) 72, (4) 110, (6) 120, (7)
60, (8) 81, (10) 64, (12) 48;
down – (2) 21, (3) 20, (5) 100, (6) 108,
(9) 16, (11) 44

14 ✔, ✗, ✗, ✔, ✗, ✗, ✔, ✔

15 4, 9, 2, 8, 3

Page 53

16 6, 48, 35, 18, 24, 84, 14, 15, 20, 36, 18,
32, 20, 55, 11, 12, 14, 18, 30, 21, 99,
48, 90, 90, 36, 54, 60, 132, 4, 8, 45, 72,
50, 63, 56, 22, 36, 42, 28, 80, 144, 27,
72, 15, 12, 108, 9, 28

Times tables charts

One times table

1	×	1	=	1
2	×	1	=	2
3	×	1	=	3
4	×	1	=	4
5	×	1	=	5
6	×	1	=	6
7	×	1	=	7
8	×	1	=	8
9	×	1	=	9
10	×	1	=	10
11	×	1	=	11
12	×	1	=	12

Two times table

1	×	2	=	2
2	×	2	=	4
3	×	2	=	6
4	×	2	=	8
5	×	2	=	10
6	×	2	=	12
7	×	2	=	14
8	×	2	=	16
9	×	2	=	18
10	×	2	=	20
11	×	2	=	22
12	×	2	=	24

Three times table

1	×	3	=	3
2	×	3	=	6
3	×	3	=	9
4	×	3	=	12
5	×	3	=	15
6	×	3	=	18
7	×	3	=	21
8	×	3	=	24
9	×	3	=	27
10	×	3	=	30
11	×	3	=	33
12	×	3	=	36

Four times table

1	×	4	=	4
2	×	4	=	8
3	×	4	=	12
4	×	4	=	16
5	×	4	=	20
6	×	4	=	24
7	×	4	=	28
8	×	4	=	32
9	×	4	=	36
10	×	4	=	40
11	×	4	=	44
12	×	4	=	48

Times tables charts

Five times table

1	×	5	=	5
2	×	5	=	10
3	×	5	=	15
4	×	5	=	20
5	×	5	=	25
6	×	5	=	30
7	×	5	=	35
8	×	5	=	40
9	×	5	=	45
10	×	5	=	50
11	×	5	=	55
12	×	5	=	60

Six times table

1	×	6	=	6
2	×	6	=	12
3	×	6	=	18
4	×	6	=	24
5	×	6	=	30
6	×	6	=	36
7	×	6	=	42
8	×	6	=	48
9	×	6	=	54
10	×	6	=	60
11	×	6	=	66
12	×	6	=	72

Seven times table

1	×	7	=	7
2	×	7	=	14
3	×	7	=	21
4	×	7	=	28
5	×	7	=	35
6	×	7	=	42
7	×	7	=	49
8	×	7	=	56
9	×	7	=	63
10	×	7	=	70
11	×	7	=	77
12	×	7	=	84

Eight times table

1	×	8	=	8
2	×	8	=	16
3	×	8	=	24
4	×	8	=	32
5	×	8	=	40
6	×	8	=	48
7	×	8	=	56
8	×	8	=	64
9	×	8	=	72
10	×	8	=	80
11	×	8	=	88
12	×	8	=	96

Times tables charts

Nine times table

1	×	9	=	9
2	×	9	=	18
3	×	9	=	27
4	×	9	=	36
5	×	9	=	45
6	×	9	=	54
7	×	9	=	63
8	×	9	=	72
9	×	9	=	81
10	×	9	=	90
11	×	9	=	99
12	×	9	=	108

Ten times table

1	×	10	=	10
2	×	10	=	20
3	×	10	=	30
4	×	10	=	40
5	×	10	=	50
6	×	10	=	60
7	×	10	=	70
8	×	10	=	80
9	×	10	=	90
10	×	10	=	100
11	×	10	=	110
12	×	10	=	120

Eleven times table

1	×	11	=	11
2	×	11	=	22
3	×	11	=	33
4	×	11	=	44
5	×	11	=	55
6	×	11	=	66
7	×	11	=	77
8	×	11	=	88
9	×	11	=	99
10	×	11	=	110
11	×	11	=	121
12	×	11	=	132

Twelve times table

1	×	12	=	12
2	×	12	=	24
3	×	12	=	36
4	×	12	=	48
5	×	12	=	60
6	×	12	=	72
7	×	12	=	84
8	×	12	=	96
9	×	12	=	108
10	×	12	=	120
11	×	12	=	132
12	×	12	=	144

Notes

Check your progress

- Shade in the stars on the progress certificate to show how much you did. Shade one star for every ⭐ you circled in this book.
- If you have shaded fewer than 20 stars go back to the pages where you circled Some ☆ or Most ⭐ and try those pages again.
- If you have shaded 20 or more stars, well done!

Collins Easy Learning Times Tables bumper book Ages 7–11
Progress certificate

to

name _____   date _____

pages 4–5	pages 6–7	pages 8–9	pages 10–11	pages 12–13	pages 14–15	pages 16–17	pages 18–19	pages 20–21
1	2	3	4	5	6	7	8	9

pages 22–23	pages 24–25	pages 26–27	pages 28–29	pages 30–31	pages 32–33	pages 34–35	pages 36–37	pages 38–39
10	11	12	13	14	15	16	17	18

pages 40–41	pages 42–43	pages 44–45	pages 46–47	pages 48–49	pages 50–51	pages 52–53
19	20	21	22	23	24	25